Shamanism and Spirituality in Therapeutic Practice

workbook

Shamanism and Spirituality in Therapeutic Practice

Christa Mackinnon

Copyright © Christa Mackinnon 2017

All rights reserved. Except for the quotation of short passages for the purposes of criticism or review, no part of this publication may be reproduced, stored in a retrieval system, or transmitted by any means, electronic, mechanical, photocopying or otherwise, without the prior written permission of the copyright holder.

First published in 2017 by

Christa Mackinnon

www.christamackinnon.com

Contents

Introduction	7
Basic Skills and Tools	9
Working with Spirit: Calling the Spirit Forces	11
A Sense of the Sacred	12
Working with Space	14
Sacredness and Wholeness of the Client	16
Axis Mundi, Cosmic Worlds & Levels of Human Perception	18
Spirit Allies	21
The Shamanic Journey	24
Journeys of Retrieval and Connection	30
Journeys of Learning or Guidance	31
Soul Loss and Soul Retrieval	32
Ceremony and Ritual	35
The Medicine Wheel: Life in Circles and Cycles	42
The Human Aspects of the Wheel: Four Directions	44
The Circle	47
The Diagonals	48
The Human Wheel: Eight Directions	50
Widening the Circle: Ancestors	52
Travelling Home: Re-Connecting with Nature	58
Connecting with the Spirits of Nature	63
Daily Nature Exercises at Home	65

Introduction

This workbook has been designed to accompany my book *Shamanism and Spirituality in Therapeutic Practice*.

The workbook is not designed to replace the book as it neither offers the profound understanding of shamanism, its cosmology, development and practical tools you will gain from reading the book, nor does it provide the background knowledge outlined in the book that enables therapeutic professionals to incorporate shamanic approaches and tools into contemporary therapeutic practice.

The workbook covers the basic practical applications from part II of the book, which I had originally designed as course Notes for therapeutic professionals who have been attending my CPD course *Bridging the Worlds: Shamanism for Therapeutic Professionals*. Only after students told me that they would find a **workbook** that only contains the practical applications helpful, have I decided that this would indeed be a useful tool for therapists and others who want to utilise approaches and exercises from the book *Shamanism and Spirituality in Therapeutic Practice*.

The workbook offers a more structured and easy access to such exercises and tools, but without in-depths background descriptions, case studies, references, examples and explanations, which the reader can find throughout the book.

The exercises in the workbook are best used in conjunction with the corresponding chapters of the book, but with some practice you will find that you don't need the book any longer, being able to rely solely on the workbook.

I hope that you find it helpful and applicable in your therapeutic practice or for your personal development.

Christa Mackinnon

Basic Skills and Tools

The importance and power of your intent

In shamanism, everything begins with an intent. An intent is a kind of vision, a goal, an outcome you want to achieve. It directs the energies of what you attempt to do, as well as the 'manifesting energies of the outcome'. It therefore needs to be formulated clearly, held attentively and absorbed into your being and into your task. The real power of your intent lies in the fact that it bridges the ordinary and non-ordinary realities. It influences the energetic worlds and therefore also the manifestation in this reality. Or, in other words, your intent is, at its most powerful, the overlap point of the goal you have and its manifestation.

Receptivity and deep listening

All spiritual practice requires us to be receptive, to be silent and listen deeply, with all our senses. No matter if you are on a shamanic journey, connect to nature, ask for help from spirit, conduct a ceremony or just want to know what you feel or intuit, or what 'spirit tells you', you have to be receptive. This means to be still enough to actually hear, see and feel what is happening on deeper levels of reality. In shamanism it is essential to understand that we cannot hear the voice of spirit if we do not listen.

Altering your state and working with spirit

All shamanic work takes place in altered states and with spirit. This means that most of the time you will use some means to go into a (light) trance state, or to assist your client to go into a light trance state. All shamanic work also requires the presence of spirit, which is called in at the beginning of shamanic endeavours. Done with focus it will tune you into deeper levels, open sacred space and bring in the energies required.

Developing trust when working with energies

As you begin shamanic practices you will have to develop a sense for energies and trust in whatever you experience, feel or sense and how it translates itself for you into images, words or intuitive knowing. For instance, you will experience whatever happens on an energetic level as images, emotions, sudden insights or thoughts, but sometimes also just as a kind of knowing or in energy forms, such as swirling or geometrical patterns, colours or strong forces. Keep in mind that you are working with energies and that the way they present or translate themselves is right for you if you have set it up in the correct way. The same applies to your client.

Vibrational tools in shamanism

Vibrations are very important in shamanism and therefore drums, rattles and sound are used for many purposes to create various levels of vibrations, such as to seal sacred space, to call in spirit forces, or for healing, journeying, trance dancing, ceremony and more. For more information please consult the appropriate chapter in the book.

Working with Spirit: Calling the Spirit Forces

Shamans, although they know their craft and have refined their skills, state that it is spirit that works with and through them. Therefore, no matter what you are doing – journeying, creating a ceremony, healing, trance dancing, dreaming, questing for vision or connecting with nature – it is important to ask spirit to be with you.

I will give you some guidance during the course as how to call in spirit for specific tasks. But, generally speaking, in shamanism we often call

1. The spirits of the four directions
2. All there is above and all there is below and Great Spirit (Great Mystery)
3. Ancestral spirits, if appropriate
4. The spirits of our 'relations' (such as nature or animal spirits), if appropriate
5. The spirit allies and helpers that can support us in a specific task.

Exercise: Basic 'spirit call'

Calling spirit with heartfelt sincerity and focus, speaking the calls aloud, is more important than trying to adhere to a set ritual or formula. You can use the following for almost everything and adjust it to your task.

1. **East** I call the powers of the East, the spirit of sun, of light, illumination, creativity
2. **South** I call the powers of the South, the spirit of water and the plant kingdom, of trust and flowing
3. **West** I call the powers of the West, the spirit of mother earth, of introspection, of the dream lodge
4. **North** I call the powers of the North, the spirit of air and the animal kingdom, of wisdom, clarity and discernment
5. **Above and Below** I call all there is above and all there is below and Great Spirit to be with us (me) during (e.g. this ceremony) so that all we (I) do, is not only for my/our own good, but for the greater good of All.

A Sense of the Sacred

Shamanic work involves working with energies and developing a feel for those underlying energetic fields, especially to develop a sense of – and for – the sacred, and to strive to bring it actively into your life and into your work with clients.

Creating an altar

A good way to begin is to create an altar, a space that is sacred for you and which you dedicate to your connection with sprit. In shamanism, an altar or mesa is a physical home for spirit and a threshold between the worlds. The objects on an altar are more than symbolic representations. They hold the very energy and power of that which they represent. For instance, when the shaman invites certain spirits to attend a ceremony, it is believed that their energies reside in the objects on the altar for the time of the ceremony.

Your personal altar holds your spiritual intent and is a place of your connection to spirit, a focal point for the sacred in your life. It assists you in your spiritual undertaking, be it meditation, a ritual, a ceremony, a quest or healing. An altar is not static, although a basic structure – such as a wheel - is often observed and the basic objects often stay the same. But generally speaking a shamanic altar is alive. It will be adjusted, depending on the work you will be doing and it will, over time, take on a life of its own. Your altar should be personal and meaningful to you.

What you need to create a basic altar

1. **A cloth** a piece of fabric that is beautiful and meaningful to you.
2. **A centrepiece** most people use a candle, signifying 'that, which always was and will always be'.
3. **The four directions of the wheel** leaving a bit of distance around the centrepiece, build up the four directions. I use crystals and stones, one in each direction: the east (a red calcite), south (a blue crystal), west (an obsidian) and north (a clear quartz).
4. **The four elements** I also include the four elements in my basic structure. To represent water, I have a small shell. A beautiful feather represents air. A tea

light in front of a small Buddha statue given to me by my daughter represents fire, while flowers or small branches represent earth.

5. **Other power objects** besides a basic altar, you can add power objects. When you work with a client you can for instance represent the client.

Exercise: Create a basic altar

Take some time to construct your altar. Be aware that you can change it, but don't wait for 'all the right objects' to show up before you start. If you can find a cloth you like, a candle for the centre and four stones to mark the four directions, you can get started. From there your altar will grow naturally.

1. **Cleanse** the objects you want to put on the altar.

2. **Call in spirit** Then state your intent – namely, creating an altar – and ask spirit to infuse your altar with beneficial energy.

3. **Infuse your objects with your intent** Next, take each object into your hands before putting it on the altar, and ask spirit to accept this as (intent: whatever it represents). Hold it for a while and energise it with your intent. Energising the object is important because your objects will, over time, turn into power objects. Speak the intent aloud when you place it on the altar. Do this with each object.

4. **Seal in the energy** Afterwards, drum or rattle around the altar space (or use whatever else feels right) to seal the energy into the space and then sit for a while, meditating on your creation. You might find that you already get some ideas about putting more on the altar, or taking something away, or that a piece on the altar begins to 'speak to you'. Be creative.

5. **Give thanks** Finally, thank spirit for their help and ask for their blessing for your altar.

Remember that the items on your altar are there to be containers of spirit. They hold the very energy of what they represent and are to be used and worked with.

Working with Space

Space, like everything else, has power. It either supports you or it doesn't. Paying attention to the energies in the space that surrounds you is really beneficial to your well-being and your spiritual connection. In shamanism, clearing/cleansing a person's energy body or a space is usually done with smoke. The easiest way to do this is to use either sage or sweet grass. You light it in a bowl, blow out the flame and use a feather to distribute the smoke. If you don't like the smell of those, use incense or, if you dislike smoke, use a sage spray.

Exercise: Cleansing your space

1. **Sensing the energy** When entering the space you work in, close your eyes for a minute or two and ask yourself the question: does the energy support my work (with my client) or not? If you feel a slight discomfort, ask: is the energy too heavy or too 'ungrounded'. Trust what comes to your mind. You will know it instinctively.

2. **Call in spirit** Keep this simple: "I call spirit to help me to clear the space."

3. **State your intent** Then state your intent aloud: "I am cleansing the space so that all the work which will be done here will be beneficial to my clients and to me. I ask spirit to help me."

4. **Cleanse** Then just walk around and smudge / spray the space. Pay attention to what you sense. Some corners need more than others; some rooms need a second round of cleansing. State your intent as often as it feels right; hold it with your mind as well as your heart, and ask for spirit's help as often as feels necessary.

Beneficial room content

You can influence how clear and focussed you and your client are by clearing your space. Clutter takes you away from what is important: that which lies beneath. I have worked in clinics where the energy was too clinical and 'cold', which is unfavourable to deeper work, as it doesn't support a 'holding environment'. I have also seen consulting rooms that were cluttered with angels and fairies and crystals, leading to a feeling of overload and chaos. When we open our minds to the subtle energies that work upon us, we begin to pay attention to what we want the room to do. If our overall intent is clarity, focus, harmony, holding and sacredness, we will create a space that expresses those intents.

Exercise: Beneficial room content

1. Stand in the middle of your consulting room and look around. Ask yourself honestly: what do I want this room to do for my client and for myself?

2. This will give you the intent of your room. Write it down.

3. Now ask the question: which content of the room does support my intent? Add or remove everything in the room that doesn't support your intent.

Sacredness and Wholeness of the Client

When we talk about concepts such as consciousness, essence, or spirit underlying all of creation and begin to comprehend that we are all part of a whole that is expressing itself, the question of how we treat everything within this 'whole' becomes essential. Just as Buddhists try to see the Buddha nature in everybody, shamanic practitioners are asked to see spirit and sacredness at the core of all living beings.

When we work as therapists, we connect with another human being's emotions, thoughts, behaviours and sensations. We encounter his longings, his passions, his hurts, his disappointments, his anger, his love, his light and his shadow, his dreams, his beauty and his darkness. We work with a human being that longs for connection, meaning, purpose, sense and self-realisation. As all life is in essence spirit revealing itself in different forms, with an innate drive to express this to the highest level possible, the ancient healer will strive to be aware of this essence field of possibilities that wants to reveal itself to the highest level possible.

It is astonishing how our whole way of working changes when we keep this idea of a sacred essence field firmly embedded in our minds. The shaman knows that the outer is influenced by the inner and vice versa and that, within this interplay, his state of mind and intent influence the person he works with. So, with the idea of the sacredness of all life embedded in her consciousness, the shamanic practitioner works in a way that gives the client the feeling of being sacred, of being a spirit in a body, of being much more than the symptoms they present with.

Exercise: Connect with your own 'sacredness' and being 'whole in essence'

1. Close your eyes before seeing clients, connect with the idea that 'all life is spirit revealing itself in different forms and therefore whole and sacred'

2. Take a few deep breaths.

3. Become still and begin to invisage yourself as being sacred. See yourself as being sacred and, in essence, whole.

4. Use all your senses: see your self as being in essence whole, feel how that

feels, hear yourself expressing from that wholeness and imagine that this essense radiates from you.

Exercise: Connect with the sacredness and wholeness of your client

Once you have connected with your own sacredness and wholeness, do the same for your client. You can use the same format as above.

1. Close your eyes and visualise the client as being sacred, and, in essence, already whole.

2. Use all your senses to experience this client as being sacred and already whole.

3. Check that you a sense of the client's wholeness in essence and a kidn of knowing that he/she is part of the sacredness of all life.

Axis Mundi, Cosmic Worlds & Levels of Human Perception

The axis mundi, also known as the cosmic axis, the cosmic tree and the centre of the world, is seen as a central axis that runs from the Earth to the sky, connecting the worlds. We find it in one form or another in almost all religions, philosophies and ancient cultures. It can take the form of places, such as mountains and hills, or images, such as trees, vines, pillars and staffs, and sometimes we find man-made structures, such as temples and pyramids, built in places that are seen as centres of the earth.

The central idea around the cosmic tree – often depicted with a solid trunk, wide-spread branches that reach into the sky and roots that reach deep into the Earth – has remained the same over time and in various cultures. It connects the three worlds or cosmic zones: the upper, middle and lower worlds, or the sky, earth and underworlds. These three worlds are also the planes of consciousness accessible via altered states. In shamanism we can pass through an opening in the cosmic tree and travel to all worlds and all times.

The three basic cosmic levels – the upper, lower and middle worlds, connected via the cosmic tree – are non-linear, timeless and infinite. They exist independently of the human mind but also form the different planes of human consciousness. Together they make up 'the whole'.

The lower and upper worlds are energetic realities, sometimes called non-ordinary realities, which we are rarely aware of in normal waking consciousness but which can be accessed in altered states. The middle world is twofold: it consists of both the invisible energetic aspects of the everyday world we live in and the visible material aspects of it. The following is a brief description of the lower and upper worlds, which we work with on this course.

The lower world

The lower world, or underworld, is mostly pictured as a landscape, with mountains, deserts, forests, rivers, oceans, caves, valleys, jungles or combinations of these. It is the home of the spirits of animals, trees, plants and rocks, as well as human-like spirits that are connected to the mystery of the Earth. The lower world is also concerned with the human psyche: our cut-off shadow aspects can be found there and our split-off soul parts will mostly flee there. The stories of the underworld are myths and fairy tales, mostly involving an encounter with a dark force. Frightening, devious, evil or monstrous beings can populate the lower world of the shaman's clients, be they individuals or the community.

Shamans work regularly in the lower world and have extensive knowledge of it. They, and indigenous people in general, own the whole – the dark and the light – and they have devised many ways and means, such as rituals, prayers, journeys and soul retrieval, to work with them and transform and integrate them.

The lower world is accessed via a journey through an imagined opening or portal into the Earth in the form of the roots of the cosmic tree, a tunnel, a hole in the ground, a well or anything that leads down. The knowing that we receive when we access the lower worlds, for instance via a shamanic journey or ceremonial means, is more instinctual than intellectual, providing us with images, sudden insights, emotional reactions, energetic forces and – quite an important aspect in all the worlds – it will be shown and taught to us by our spirit helpers. The spirit helpers of the lower world appear mainly in the form of power animals.

The upper world

The upper world(s) appear and feel different from the lower world. They often appear as etheric realms of many layers. The light is brighter here, colours are usually more pastel and somehow fuzzy, and the whole place feels quite airy. Crystal structures, cloudlike realms and cosmic beings can be encountered.

The upper world is traditionally accessed via the branches of the cosmic tree, ropes, staircases leading upwards, high mountains, rainbows or smoke. It is inhabited by helping spirits, powerful teachers in humanoid form, formless spirit beings and ancestral spirits.

In the upper world we seek guidance and wisdom, and what we perceive and receive is not instinctual, but rather has philosophical and wise qualities in the sense that it is knowledge that seems to reach beyond 'what we know'.

In the upper world we can connect with our spirit guides and teachers and our ancestors in spirit form. Some contemporary shamanic teachers also recommend we look for our own 'higher self' within those realms. This is our transpersonal aspect, sometimes also called the over-soul, the immortal aspect of ourselves that can communicate with us through dreams and visions and be a source of intuition, inspiration and guidance.

The four levels of human perception

Four hierarchically ordered levels of human perception. There are slightly different animal representations of these levels in various cultures, but as the animals represent the energies of the levels, their appearance is of minor importance.

1. **The physical level is represented by the Serpent.** It is our body, our instinctual knowing and our senses. This level guides us when the sensual and instinctual are required. It knows nature, danger and opportunity. It is also the level where we act physically in a physical world. It is the level of beta brainwaves, where our brain is active in an outwardly focused way in the waking state.

2. **The mental/emotional level is represented by the Jaguar.** It is the level where we feel and think. The Jaguar is a great hunter, stalking its prey, planning its route and changing quickly when required to ensure a successful hunt. It represents our mental capacity, enabling us to plan, think, be emotionally involved and bring our visions and dreams to fruition in the material world. When we focus inwardly and enter the alpha state and can bring this level more fully to our awareness.

3. **The soul level is represented by the Hummingbird**, which is aware of our soul's journey. This is the level we are on when we are on a profound shamanic journey or very deeply immersed in ceremonial work. Here we can create, have visions and encounter spirits. On this level our intent has great power and we are the energetic co-creators we are meant to be. We can experience this level when we are in theta – when we are in a deep trance state.

4. **The spirit level is represented by the Eagle**. It is the domain of spirit, the realm where everything already exists in potential form. This is knowing on the highest level and in shamanic terms we do not need to change anything here, because the bigger picture is shown to us and all is well. We are at the level of 'Oneness', of just Being. Some call it the level of enlightenment. Ourbrain sinks down into delta waves or even lower, to a state where we hardly exist but are one with the whole.

We are asked to become aware at which level we are functioning: we use our senses and instincts on the physical level, be aware of our mental and emotional capacities and states and use them wisely on that level, to dream and create on the level of soul and, on the spirit level, to become aware of our soul's path and strive to expand our consciousness to reach the highest level of knowing.

Spirit Allies

There is no shamanic work without spirit allies and teachers. These provide the shaman with power, wisdom, guidance, teaching, help and protection in the various worlds, especially in the spirit world. In shamanism we strive for a strong, reciprocal relationship with spirit allies.

Power animals

Power animals are helping and guardian spirits best described as being 'the essence of a species perceived in the form of an animal'. They are essential for many tasks the shaman undertakes, such as lower/underworld journeys, healing, shapeshifting, ceremony and soul retrieval.

In shamanism animal spirits are seen as manifestations of a natural power that is stronger, and often wiser, than human beings. When we are in touch with animal spirits, we are stronger and more likely to be in touch with our own nature as well as the natural world, and therefore less disconnected and fragmented.

In some cultures it is assumed that the spirits of at least two power animals stay with us from birth to keep us physically safe and healthy and that losing a power animal is one of the causes of illness and the retrieval of power animals via journeying is seen as vital to restore health. Certain North American indigenous cultures distinguish between four types of animal guide: journey guides accompany and help us through a certain part of our life's journey; messenger guides leave us as soon as the message is understood: shadow animal guides infuse us with fear, returning at times in our lives when we are severely tested; other guides stay with us over a lifetime.

It is important to recognize that we do not choose our power animal. It will come to us and it is for us to accept it, learn from it, work with it and build a relationship with it. All power animals are equal, as they are part of the energy of the divine in nature and our own instinctual forces. They have thus certain qualities. Each provides a specific kind of medicine, which, let me assure you, will be exactly the one your client needs. For instance, a male participant in one of my groups who was very introverted and shy connected with a roaring black bear, whilst a woman who had real problems with her own femininity connected with an otter – a very feminine water energy – and a client of mine who was heavy and whose soul was starved connected with a hummingbird.

Although more than a psychological metaphor, power animals are also helpful in many ways psychologically: they are balanced creatures and having the energy of a power animal around is helpful with difficult emotional states because they are usually nurturing, loving, generous in their help and regard you positively. These qualities are in themselves healing forces.

It is difficult to describe the relationship with your power animal. It needs building and nurturing and one has to experience it, rather than being taught. In comparison to spirit guides, power animals are not very verbal. Instead, they communicate by taking you to places and showing you things. They are not your instinct, but they certainly activate it.

Upper-world teachers and guides

Not all schools of shamanism distinguish spirit guides or upper-world teachers from ancestral spirits, animal spirits and other spirits of the non-material invisible worlds. But, as the distinction between the upper and lower worlds gives us a structure, we can say that spirit teachers and guides are often seen as spirits of the upper world that appear to us in humanoid or symbolic form.

Guides and teachers can be spirit entities that have been in a body, such as ancestral spirits, or that have never been in human form. As beings of the upper world, they are of a different vibration, having a mostly ethereal, cosmic quality, and their gifts have a quality of universal wisdom. They are the allies who can help us to see the bigger picture and who often answer questions, guide us, assist us and teach us about subjects concerned with soul, sense, purpose and meaning, but they also assist in healing, divination, ceremony and the energetic work we do in the different worlds.

Shamans often have several such allies, with different qualities, roles and functions. They can be acquired through journeying, plant journeys, initiation ceremonies, extreme altered state experiences or dreaming. Most importantly, as has already been emphasized, there can be no shamanic work without a strong relationship to spirit allies. I work with three upper-world guides whom I know quite well, but other guides show up at various times.

Guides are available to everybody. All you need to do to make contact with them is to be open and ask serenely. To have a power animal in place is in many cases enough to begin your shamanic work, but it is beneficial to learn how to communicate with upper-world teachers and to find an upper-world ally.

Therapists who include shamanic practices and tools into their work are advised to help clients to connect early in the process with their spirit allies as it is beneficial for clients to have access to power animals, guides and teachers as helping and guiding forces throughout the therapeutic process as well as in their daily lives. The best way to establish this connection is via the shamanic journey, which will be introduced in the next chapter.

The Shamanic Journey

The shamanic journey is a way to travel into the different worlds - the lower, upper and middle worlds. The realms of those worlds are traditionally utilised to find the source of the problem and the path of the resolution, such as which ritual or ceremony to perform, which herbs to use, which spirits to get involved or which soul parts to bring back. The journey is furthermore used for divination as well as for different forms of energetic healing within those worlds.

Journeying is used by many different practitioners, including therapists and psychologists, some of whom might define the field we access when we journey as being the 'personal unconscious or the collective unconscious'.

The traditional journey adapted in contemporary shamanism is 20 – 30 minutes long and usually accompanied by a steady drum-rhythm. When journeying is used in a consulting room with clients, it can also be treated like any process-orientated therapeutic work. When I treat it like a process, I use a brief hypnotic induction, leading the client to his/her sacred place and begin the journey from there. Used in such a way, I found it more beneficial to let the journey run for as long as it takes to come to a natural end, usually in form of an adequate insight, solution, shift of belief or other conclusion.

The journey is an unfolding process and a journey's content and context can be complex and multi-layered, but they are usually coherent and the content is consistent with the purpose/intent of the journey. Thus much of the therapist's work during the journey is to listen to the narrative without interrupting or interpreting and only sometimes, if necessary, to prompt or remind the client to repeat the intent and to ask their power animals and spirit guides for help.

Contemporary practitioners use the shamanic journey for many different reasons. You can use it to connect with power animals, spirit guides and spirits in general. One can journey to find something one needs to let go off, retrieve split-off parts and soul parts in general, reveal the root cause of an issue or problem, discover solutions, receive advice, untangle emotional webs, heal emotional wounding, find out about relationships and more. We can also journey to receive learning about a range of things, such as our task in this world, our shadows, our spiritual selves, our connection with our ancestors, our essence qualities and so on.

The structure of a shamanic journey

A journey is always conducted in the same way:

1. The intent is clearly defined (and stated a few times at the beginning of the journey)
2. Spirit is called in
3. A starting place from which to travel is visualised
4. A designation of the world to which the client wants to journey is stated (upper, lower or middle world)
5. The help of a power animal and/or guide is requested
6. Once this is set up, both, the client and the therapist are asked to trust the process completely, rather than trying to interfere, direct or interpret.
7. The vehicles used throughout shamanic journeying to lead the brain into an altered state are drums, rattles or any sounds that produces the vibration of the theta state of the brain. In a therapeutic environment one can also utilise a 'trance induction' or other means.
8. The most used shamanic journey is 20 to 30 minutes long. Again, in a therapeutic environment, it is advised to let the journey come to its natural conclusion, rather than setting a time frame.
9. The journey will come to a natural conclusion and/or a 'calling up' beat or techique is employed

As a general rule of thumb, journeys of a 'psychological nature' lead into the lower world. Journeys that are of a connecting with spiritual/higher self states or ask for guidance from those realms usually lead to the upper world.

Defining the intent

Define, together with your client, a precise intent such as:

I am going to journey to connect with my power animal

I am going to journey to get advise about (insert appropriately)

I am going to journey to help me decide about my relationship

I am going to journey to find the root cause of my (insert appropriately; for example, self-sabotage, depressive tendency, anxiety) and what would help me to overcome it.

I am going to journey to retrieve (insert appropriately)

I am going to journey to find out what I need to let go to achieve (insert appropriately)

I am going to journey into the upper world to find/learn about my essence

I am going to journey to the upper world find my place of one-ness

Setting up and accompanying a client during a journey

Use the trance induction, leading your client to her sanctuary/power place or use a drumming CD.

1. In the special place, instruct your client to find a way to travel into the earth (for lower world journeys) or to travel upwards (for upper world journeys). Ask for confirmation that she has found a way to do that and instruct her to state her intent at least three or four times, preferably aloud 'I am going to journey into the lower world to ... (intent) ... and I ask my power animal and spirit guide to help me.'

2. Instruct your client to use her imagination to travel 'down' and just be guided by the images, feelings or/and sensations. Instruct your client to let the journey unfold.

3. Ask you client to narrate the journey to you – where is she, what is going on, what is happening next. If you want to ask questions during the journey, keep them open ended, non-directive and neutral. If at all necessary I tend to ask 'what is happening now?'

4. Let the process take over. Detach from any expectations with regards to the process or the outcome.

5. If your client gets stuck, travels 'all over the place' or experiences very strong feelings, ask her to state her intent again, to ask for help, to ask her power animal or guide to show her the way and so on. Do not interrupt the journey.

6. When the journey has come to its conclusion (don't worry – you and your client will know), instruct your client to bring back whatever she needs/

wants to bring back and count from 10-1, telling your client that whilst you are counting she will come back to her special place, and then back to the 'here and now' in your consulting room. Ask her to thank her power animal and guide for their help as she travels back to normal waking reality and then, after counting, ask her to open her eyes. If you use a drumming CD there will be a 'coming back beat' which is distinctly different from the 'trance beat'.

7. After this, process what has been happening during the journey with the means you usually employ: talk about the journey if necessary; find an affirmation if appropriate; craft an energy container that symbolises whatever needs letting go and burn it, instruct your client to write the journey down as homework and to reflect upon it, do some integrative work etc.

8. If you have called in spirit and created a sacred space, don't forget to thank spirit afterwards.

Exercise: Journey to establish the place of power

Use the drumming download and the journey outline above

1. Your intent is: "*I am journeying to the lower world to find and connect with my power place. I ask spirit to help me.*"

2. Follow steps 1 to 5 (described above)

3. Travel down. You will arrive in a landscape. Observe it; explore it; get a feel for it. There might be a special area or place to which you feel drawn. Sit there for a while. You can change your power place by adding or removing things.

4. When you hear the call-up beat, come back (see point 12 above) and write the journey down.

Exercise: Journey to connect with a power animal

Use the drumming download and the journey outline above

1. Your intent is: "*I am going to journey into the lower world to meet my power animal.*"

2. Imagine that you are travelling down into the lower world.

3. You will end up in your place of power, where you will meet an animal. Turn away from it a few times. If you meet it repeatedly, ask it if it is your power animal.

4. When you have met your power animal, let the journey unfold. Observe the animal; get to know its energy, its qualities. Be with it; let the animal lead.

5. When you hear the call-up beat, thank your animal and ask it if it wants to come with you. Bring it with you, travelling up the same way as you travelled down.

6. Thank spirit and your animal.

Integrating the power animal with your client

The power animal often either has qualities the client needs to incorporate more into his life or qualities that need to come more to the forefront. Discuss the qualities of the power animal and associations your client has with that specific animal. It is astonishing how much the client will learn about himself. Once your client has made contact with the power animal, you should incorporate it as a helping spirit into all shamanically-orientated work. It can also be used when needing guidance, especially when it comes to splits between the head and the heart, the instinctual and the rational. What the power animal advises reflects the instinctual. Power animals are also fantastic helpers when it comes to emotionally charged states, inner child work, ego-state work, regressions and soul retrieval. The power animal can be brought into the therapeutic work as a helping spirit at any time.

Exercise: Journey to Connect with a Spirit Guide

Use the drumming download and the journey outline above

1. Intent: "*I am going to journey to the upper world to meet my spirit teacher.*"

2. Imagine that you are travelling upwards. Be aware that you need to travel through layers and that the layers often become increasingly ethereal, hazier. Let the journey unfold.

3. You will meet teachers/guides in humanoid or symbolic form. Ask whomever you meet if he/she is your teacher/guide. When you have met your teacher, be with them. Spending some time with your teacher. Getting to know their qualities is important. You can ask questions or ask for advice.

4. At the end of the journey, thank the teacher or guide.

Integration work with spirit teacher

Discuss the guide with your client, if that feels appropriate, and ask for his/her qualities and wisdom. Let the client express how she feels about the guide. Instruct the client to write about the journey and the qualities of the teacher. If the teacher gave the something symbolic in answer to question or instructed them directly, make sure the advice or instruction is followed. Encourage the client to put something that symbolizes their upper world teacher on your altar. Spirit guides, as described in chapter 3, function as advisors, counsellors and helpers. They generally carry wisdom and knowledge of a higher nature and it is beneficial to call upon them whenever appropriate during therapeutic work, especially work that is emotionally painful or when a certain level of wisdom and guidance is needed.

Journeys of Retrieval and Connection

All journeys of a psychological nature can start in the lower world. Journeys into the lower world can change into middle world journeys or upper world journeys spontaneously. As long as the intent was set up correctly, helpers are called in and the procedure is followed, we need to trust that clients will end up on the level they require to complete the task.

Exercise: Journeys of connection

1. **Intent** "*I am going to journey into the lower world to find and connect with* (insert whatever the client wants to find). *I ask my power animal and guide to help me.*"
2. Imagine that you are travelling down. Make sure your power animal is with you.
3. *Follow your power animal. It will – in most cases – be your guide*
4. *Let the journey unfold. State your intent again and ask your power animal for help in case you get lost or encounter stumbling blocks during the journey.*
5. *When you are called back, bring imagine that you will bring the part you found with you.*

Exercise: Journeys to the source

Intent *I am going to journey into the lower world to find out when (insert) was created and what I can do to resolve it. I ask my power animal and spirit guide to help me.*

Exercise: Journeys of retrieval

Intent: "*I am going to journey to the lower world to retrieve a part that I need right now in my life to* (insert whatever the client wants to achieve). *I ask my power animal and guide to help me.*"

Journeys of Learning or Guidance

We can journey to 'learn about my shadow', to 'learn about one-ness' to 'learn about my connection to spirit", to 'learn about my essence', to learn about 'my tasks in life' and more. When one wants to learn something that is more universal, such as 'one-ness' or 'essence' or 'task' the journey can be set-up to lead into the upper world. In my experience though, even if you begin the journey as a lower world journey, the client will travel to the upper world if appropriate. Alternatively, you can leave it open, keeping the intent ' vague' with regards to the world: *'I am going to journey to the upper or lower world to* (insert appropriately). *I am asking my power animal and spirit guide to help me.'*

Another form to journey to get information and learn is to journey directly to a teacher. This can be the spirit guide or the power animal or the intent can be kept artfully vague *'I am going to journey to a teacher who can teach me about* (insert). *I ask my power animal and guide to help me.'* Then start the journey in the usual way and let it unfold.

Exercise: Journey to the upper world for learning

Intent *"I am going to journey to the upper world to learn about my essence. I ask for help from my power animals and guides"*

Integration of journey outcomes

The journey works on an energetic as well as cognitive level, but it is vital to integrate whatever has been retrieved, or the outcome of the exploration, with either the means described throughout my book such as ceremonial work, nature work, story writing, dance, affirmations, crafting objects, representations on altar, appropriate homework and more. As a trained therapeutic professional you can also employ your usual ways and tools of integration.

Soul Loss and Soul Retrieval

In the world of shamanism it is assumed that it is mainly the loss of soul that causes emotional, physical and mental disease and diminishes essential life energy. It is therefore seen as vital to return the soul, or parts of the soul, to the client. The description of soul loss shows remarkable similarities to what contemporary psychology calls 'dissociation' in that the shamanic concept of soul loss recognizes, like the psychological concept of dissociation, the capacity of human beings to split off parts of their psyche in response to trauma and/or adverse circumstances.

Dissociation is a device the brain uses to survive potentially destructive traumatic events. It minimizes perception and later, if the event isn't processed adaptively, it can block access to cognitive, sensory and affective memory (or to parts of the memory). The brain uses dissociative devices furthermore to disconnect from emotional states and manifesting behaviours of those states, such as anger, rage or sadness, if they cannot be expressed without risking ongoing punishment, be it physical or emotional. A simple example is rage, which in most cultures is not accepted and can, when expressed, lead to either direct punishment or to the withdrawal of love and affection by parents. Over time we 'split off' the part of us that is raging or angry, sometimes to a point where we don't feel and accept it any longer as being a part of us.

Dissociation is an adaptive response, enabling us to survive situations that threaten our life, or psychological integrative self, which turns maladaptive over time as it hinders integration. The long term price to pay for non-integration of traumatic material or emotionally unacceptable states can be developmental arrest, the manifestation of those defenses and parts in distressing, debilitating and incapacitating ways such as anxieties, depression, addictions and compulsions as well as a loss of part of our energies, and our psychological and mental potential.

Both, contemporary psychology and shamanic concepts, understand that dissociation takes place, but whilst contemporary thinking would locate dissociated parts and states within the mind, the shaman defines soul loss as a spiritual illness and believes that the dissociated parts can 'flee the body' and hide somewhere outside, in the case of soul loss mainly in the lower world.

Although it is now widely accepted that we can only dissociate when we alter our state in the way our brain manages for instance instantly and automatically when confronted with a potentially traumatic situation, it is not accepted within psychological thinking that such energies could have been split off to an extent that they have become inaccessible, unless somebody who is trained in working in parallel and 'other worlds' accesses them for us. Besides hiding in inaccessible realms, those parts are, in shamanic thinking, also guarded by heavy defenses, which are difficult or impossible for the affected person to overcome. During the shamanic journey to retrieve soul parts we indeed encounter quite strong energies, which often show themselves as monsters, reptiles, dragons and other dangerous beasts. They literally guard the split-off soul. The shamanic practitioner will have to overcome those, mainly with the help of spirit helpers, and persuade the soul part to come back. The persuasion of the part is necessary because it is arrested, refusing to come back to a reality that is still perceived as being dangerous.

To retrieve a soul the shaman will journey into the spirit world, accompanied by spirit helpers, with the intent to retrieve a certain part, narrating, at least in contemporary shamanism, the whole journey to the client. Once the shaman has retrieved the part he/she will re-integrate it for the client and together with the client. This is usually done firstly energetically, by blowing the energy into the body, but also with means of ceremony and now, in more contemporary practice, cognitively. In psychotherapeutic practice we would attempt a similar form of re-integration of dissociated parts or ego-states, using mainly ego-state therapy, inner child work, parts work, Gestalt approaches and other techniques, but we would not attempt to do it 'for the client' by locating the part and bringing it back. In fact, the generally accepted ethics of psychotherapy might define this level of involvement as borderline unethical or counter-productive.

Exercise: Soul Retrieval

1. Soul retrieval is done via a shamanic journey. You retrieve the part for another person. Explain the concept to the client.

2. Set-up as you would for a shamanic journey

3. Stay in contact with your client. Some people need physical contact.

4. Intent: "I am going to journey to the lower world to retrieve a part for…(name of your partner / client)… which she split off and which she needs right now. I ask my power animals and other spirit helpers to be with me and guide me" (You can formulate various intents – depending whether you look for a specific part or attempt a general retrieval).

5. Journey to the lower world in the usual way. Use you guides extensively.

6. Narrate your journey to your partner. Do neither filter nor change anything.

7. When you are shown the part you will have to ask "Is this the part I was searching for. Is it ok to bring the part back."

8. Bring the part back

9. Integrate the part

Give homework and do more integration work with the part (see above). Do not discuss the journey extensively, especially not in an analytical way, rather come back to it in the next session.

Ceremony and Ritual

Ceremony and ritual form one of the foundations of all shamanic work. They are used in all traditions to connect with the sacred and with spirit, to become aware of the different energies in and around us and to work on the level of soul. In this sense they are vehicles to make us aware of - and integrate – aspects of our multi-dimensional selves, our conscious self and our unconscious patterns with something deeper, which we can call our soul, as well as with something greater than ourselves, in shamanic terms with 'spirit'. They form a bridge between ordinary realms and the realms of the unseen, between our mind and soul, between the sacred and the mundane – and create harmony between them. Ceremony helps us to turn some of the ordinary into something sacred.

Traditionally, ceremonial work is used for healing, for rites of passage, for blessings, initiations, dedications, cleansing, for the shaman's flight and journeys, for giving something back to the earth, for expressing gratitude and for questing vision, meaning and purpose and much more.

The symbolic elements used in rituals and ceremonies are charged with meaning, eliciting powerful psychological 'whole-brain' responses. Roger Walsh, professor of psychiatry and explorer of shamanism and consciousness proposes that, at their best, shamanic healing rituals induce the full panoply of healing responses simultaneously:

1. Cultural therapy: they heal and create community

2. Socio-therapy: they repair relationships, harmonise social structures and stabilise society

3. Psychosomatic therapy: they diminish disease and its complications

4. Gene therapy: they modulate gene expression

5. Psychotherapy: they heal the subjective dis-ease of illness

6. Spiritual therapy: they relieve a sense of alienation and estrangement from the universe, create a sense of connection and alignment with the sacred and foster a transpersonal/transegoic sense of identity

The words ritual and ceremony are often used interchangeably, although, strictly speaking, rituals follow a set pattern and are repeated over time, while ceremony, being less formal, allows us to be creative and spontaneous. So the ceremonial work I will be focusing on here is based on a creative act, in the sense that we decide for what purpose we want to create a ceremony, and when and how the ceremony is performed. This way, ceremonies can be created with individual clients or with groups to suit therapeutic purposes.

In ceremony we enter into a sacred, symbolic enactment of an intent. This intense enactment elicits powerful responses within the individual psyche and the whole group, producing connection, healing, change and manifestation. Here are a few pointers as to how ceremony works:

1. Ceremony elicits holistic brain responses
2. It creates inner harmony and reduces inner conflict
3. We enter a higher state of consciousness.
4. It has meaning for our inner world and helps us to manifesting outer reality
5. Ceremonies and ritual create a powerful field, especially when done in group
6. They elicit a sense of being embedded in the transpersonal.
7. They contribute to creating a better world.

Ceremonial work within a therapeutic setting

In a contemporary therapeutic setting, ceremony lends itself to resolve issues, to speak or to hear the truth, to finish unfinished business, to celebrate an achievement, to give thanks, to send out wishes and prayers, to release or give away fear, anger or grief, or to call in something that we want to attract. Mainly it is used to integrate and consolidate work you have done during a session. No matter what the purpose of your ceremony may be, ceremonial work is transformational.

Ceremonies are fun to create, but unfortunately they lend themselves more to working with groups than with individuals and to a less time restricted setting. Nevertheless, one can use them in one-to-one sessions, as they don't have to be elaborate and can involve any number of people.

Vital components of a ceremony

1. A clearly defined and stated intent.
2. A ceremonial space
3. Spirit present
4. A symbolic representation and/or enactment (the ritual)

I have created many ceremonies over the years and have used them with individual clients and with groups. With individual clients, I usually keep them brief and to the point. The one I use most with individual clients is an adaptation of the fire ceremony, usually in the last 20 to 30 minutes of the session. I also sometimes give ceremonial work as homework, between sessions. The intent is usually determined by the outcome of the session, such as to let go of something or to call something in or integrate something. If done repeatedly between sessions to consolidate change, the ceremony can over time turn into a ritual for the client.

How to structure a basic ceremony

1. **Intent** Define the intent with your client or with a group of people.
2. **The ritual** Decide how you want to create the ritual.
3. **Define the space** I usually use stones to create a circle utilising four or eight directions (see medicine wheel). The ceremony takes place inside the circle. Anything that is available can be used as long as it clearly defines/marks the space.
4. **Call in spirit** in a way that is comfortable for you and the people you are with. Do this aloud: for example, 'I am calling in spirit to bless the ceremony we are about to do and to help us with it.' This is the simplest form. I call in the spirits of the four directions, ancestral spirits and often also also specific guides.
5. **Sacred Space** Transform the space into 'sacred space'. Cleanse it by walking around it with smudge or use sound in form of a Tibetan bell, a singing bowl, a drum or rattle. Build a little altar. A simple cloth on the floor will do. Then put on the cloth a centrepiece that represents the intent of the ceremony... a candle, some flowers, a stone or whatever else feels appropriate. When you put it on the altar, speak the intent aloud. Then have every person place an object on the altar. They can say whatever they want to say while doing that.

Last but not least, put something there to represent the spirits you want to be present. I generally use fire, water, earth and air as well as something that represents 'spirit in general'. What you use must relate to the intent, the people involved and the spirits you want present and its important to create it as 'beautiful' as you possible can with the means you have available.

6. **Stay inside the sacred space** for the remainder of the ceremony. Call in spirit again, stating your specific intent and ask for help to achieve the intent.

7. **Do the ritual**, involving everybody as much as possible.

8. **Finish.** When your ceremony is finished, do something to mark the end, for example, drum, rattle, chant or meditate for a few minutes. Do whatever feels right and supports the people and the intent. Give thanks to the spirits you have called and to other helping energies

9. **Clear the space**

10. **Walk away!** It's done. Go back to normal reality.

Exercise: Fire ceremony with individual clients

The basic idea of the fire ceremony is to burn something – sending it up to spirit – with intent (manifesting the intent).

1. **Crafting the object that holds the intent** To create this, use simple things, such as pieces of paper and colouring pens or small twigs and wool. Ask the client to use whatever they fancy to create something that symbolises what she wants to let go or call in or integrate. This can be a small drawing, a twig decorated with some wool, or some writing on a piece of paper. Set a time limit for the task, as this focuses the mind, and the client is instructed to hold the intent during the whole process of crafting.

2. **Create the circle** Build a circle, using stones. The stones are chosen by the client and laid down by me. I might burn some incense, dim the lights and light some candles whilst my client crafts the item.

3. **Call in spirit** Ask your client is asked to sit inside the circle and to close her eyes. Call in spirit with the help of a rattle or a drum or, if the energy feels heavy, with the help of a singing bowl or Tibetan bell. I tell my client that she can call in spirit or spirit helpers silently, in whatever form she would like, according to her own belief system.

4. **The Ritual** After we have invited spirit, I ask my client to hold the object, to state her intent, to really feel what she wants to let go or call in or integrate, and then I instruct her to burn the object in a bowl with a candle, which has been placed in the circle beforehand. The client is encouraged to state the intent: for instance, 'I am letting go of (insert appropriately) with thanks, asking (insert appropriately) to help me' a few times whilst she watches the object burn. After the object has burned, ask your client to close her eyes again and imagine that whatever she has just worked on is already happening.

5. **Give thanks and dismantle the circle** Give thanks to spirit, encouraging the client to do the same, silently or aloud. Dismantle the circle and end session. Do not discuss.

Exercise: Affirming and honouring aspects of ourselves

This ceremony will take a whole session and needs some preparation.

The ceremony's intent is to meet and honour four basic aspcts of oneself.

> **East** The magical spirit child
>
> **West** The inner man or woman
>
> **North** The wise adult
>
> **South** Trusting, creative playful child

The client is 'the witness' in the centre of the circle.

First round

1. Create a circle, using stones for the four directions, South, West, North and East. The space has to be large enough for the client to be able to sit in each direction, facing the centre.

2. Create sacred space by calling in spirit and defining the circle

3. The first round: your client sits in the middle, facing each direction in turn, beginning with the East. Ask your client to imagine her 'inner spirit child' in the East, stressing that the spirit child can come in all shapes and forms, but that it is magical, spirited. Ask your client to describe whatever image comes to her. Take Notes.

4. Do the same for the other three directions, stressing that these are positive

aspects, not influenced by life events.

Second round

Ask you client to sit in each specific direction. You can sit in the centre, being the witness.

1. Ask your client to begin in the East, closing her eyes, taking a few deep breaths and then remembering the image from round 1. Now ask your client to begin to embody the magical child, feeling as if she were this magical, spirit child. Ask your client to nod her head when she has a sense of being the spirit child. Now ask your client to speak starting 'I am Rosie's spirit child... I am ... [whatever comes out]' Encourage your client to speak feely, letting come what wants to come. Do not comment or judge.

2. When there is silence, ask the client to let the magical spirit child go and, in her own time, open her eyes, coming back to the circle.

3. Proceed to the South, repeating the exercise until your client has completed the circle.

4. When the client has completed the circle, and has embodied all four aspects, ask her to come back into the middle, close her eyes and silently reflect, honouring and giving thanks to her beautiful inner aspects.

5. Finish: give thanks and clear the space

Don't discus the ceremony and what happened afterwards so as not to intellectualise what should be left to work its way through the system, unless you feel that there is some integration work to be done. After a ceremony such as 'honouring the four aspects', it might be beneficial to give homework that refers back to the aspects and then, should this be the client's need, to discuss whatever needs talking about in the next session.

Exercise: Tree ceremony

This ceremony works best with groups, inside or outside, but you can use it with individual clients, especially when you address various intents within one ceremony or if you want the client to do ongoing homework with the tree.

1. **What you need** A container or vase, filled with water or sand. Make sure it is steady. Cut some branches ceremonially or collect them from the ground

– ask permission and give thanks. Have some wool or ribbons ready.

2. **Create sacred space** and call in spirit. Put the branches and the wool or ribbons into the middle of the circle.

3. **Ritual** In groups: Each participant takes it in turns to walk around the inside of the circle – clockwise or anticlockwise to build up an energy field. When they reach the tree, they cut a piece of wool and wind it around the branches, stating their intent out loud. If you do that with an individual client, find either one intent e.g. "giving thanks for the blessings in my life" or "letting go of everything that doesn't serve me any longer" or "creating the life I want to lead". Encourage the client to repeat the ritual several times, cutting a piece of wool for each aspect of the intent and hanging it on the tree, until all the aspects are covered.

4. **Finish** Give thanks, dismantle the circle and either give the branches to the client to take home or, if you created the ritual to 'let something go', burn the branches ceremonially or bury them.

The Medicine Wheel: Life in Circles and Cycles

Circle-like structures, based on nature observation, have been constructed and used all over the world as ways of depicting life in circles and cycles, organising and passing on understanding and information about the world and life, as well as sacred and ceremonial constructs and spaces to honour life and spirit.

The Medicine Wheel, also called the 'Sacred Hoop', is used by indigenous peoples of the North Americas but, as most sources state, comes originally from the Maya in South America. It is, like all ancient wheels, firstly based on nature observations, then it moves from the elegantly simple, a centre and four directions, to the increasingly complex, with the number of wheels being theoretically infinite. In its many adapted forms it is now also widely used as a tool for personal exploration and development, with most contemporary practitioners using eight directions around the wheel and a split centre.

The basic formation of the medicine wheel is based on the four compass directions - East, South, West and North - representing the powers of those directions as well as their interrelatedness. These four directions correspond with the four elements, the four seasons, the four races, the four aspects of the human – the mental, physical, emotional and spiritual - and the four stages of life. In the centre we find 'the children's fire', representing the infinite sacred mystery, which always was and always will be.

Wheels are applied to a wide variety of subjects, such as the workings of the wider universe, of earth and nature, of communities and the humanity within the whole. There are also wheels about specific human aspects such as the body, the mental/emotional, beliefs, behaviours, creativity, spirituality, development, relationships and more.

It is believed that we all carry the 'sacred hoop of life' within us and thus the directions resonate with us on a deep level. The following exercises can be used with clients.

Exercise: connecting with the 'sacred' of the four direction

1. **Create a wheel.** Use four stones or crystals or the pieces from your altar. Place them in the directions of the East (fire), West (earth), South (water) and North (air), leaving enough space for you to stand in the middle of the circle.

2. **Call in spirit**, while standing in the middle of the circle. Still yourself.

3. **Turn East** and say: "*I ask the spirits of the east to teach me about the sun and fire and how to bring the sacred of the East into my life.*"

4. **Turn South** and say: "*I ask the spirits of the south to teach me about water and the plant kingdom and how to bring the sacred of the South into my life.*"

5. **Turn West** and say "*I ask the spirits of the west to teach me about earth, about the deep mother and how to bring the sacred of the West into my life.*"

6. **Turn North** and say "*I ask the spirits of the North to teach me about air and the animal kingdom and how to bring the sacred of the North into my life.*"

7. **Finish** by thanking the spirits and dismantle the wheel

Stay in each direction for as long as it feels right and just let the teachings come to you. You will get much information and insights in the form of feelings, images and advice. Make sure you write down what you remember afterwards and find ways to 'bring the sacred of each direction' into your life.

If you do this exercise with a client, let them narrate to you the information they are receiving from each direction and write it down for them. Help them to find concrete ways and means how they can 'bring the sacred of each direction' into their lives.

The Human Aspects of the Wheel: Four Directions

The Medicine Wheel addresses all aspects, the conscious aspects and more unconscious aspects of our ego self, the dark and the light aspects of our psyche, and our soul and spirit aspects. We generally work with the wheel with the aim of integrating the aspects to the highest possible extent at any given moment. We can also use it to look at our development at each stage in our lives and our connections to universal fields. The following descriptions of the directions provide a basis for you to work with.

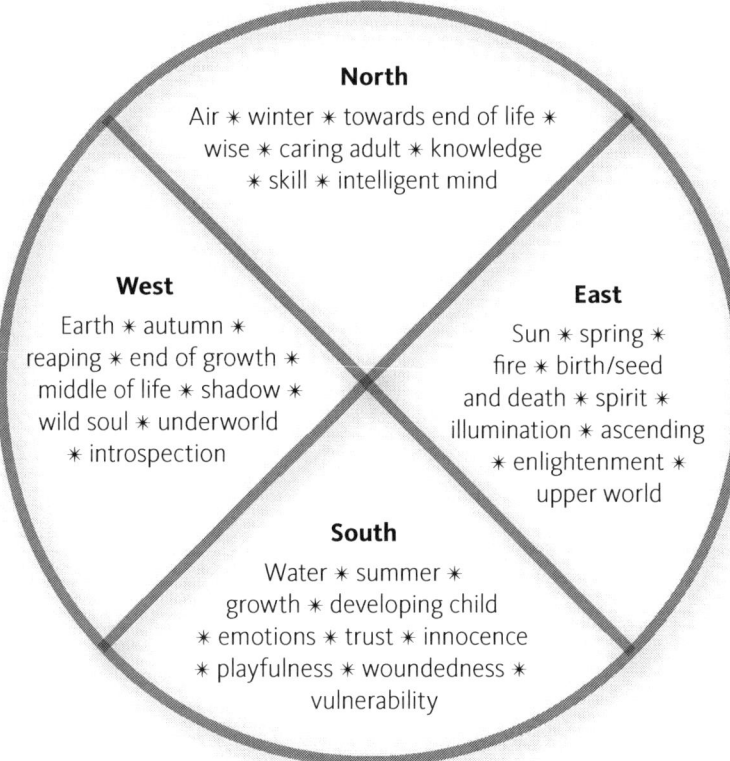

The East is the place of the sun, where it all begins and ends, the place of birth, death and rebirth. It is associated with spirit, illumination, creativity and with the upper world. The East asks us to look at our spirituality.

The South is the place of water, our emotional self: the inner child, with its beauty, innocence, playfulness and wonder, but also its wounding. The South asks us to look at our emotional self.

The West is the place of earth, the physical. It is the place of our human body and for our psyche it is the place of 'shadow', the underworld and our earth soul. The West asks us to introspect, to go deep and confront and transform our own darkness, but also to retreat and dream.

The North is the place of air. It is cold and dark. Humans need skill, knowledge, endurance and wisdom to thrive in the north. It is the place of the mental, of the adult. We are asked to 'stop the world', examine our thoughts, philosophies and beliefs and grow wise before we die.

Exercise: Getting a snapshot

This is a basic, but very effective exercise to tune into the four major aspects of oneself: the emotional, child self (South), the mental, adult self (North), the physical/manifesting self (West) and the spiritual self (East).

1. **Create a wheel**
2. **Call in Spirit** and centre yourself
3. **Turn South.** Ask: which image represents the South? How do I feel in the South? What is my task right now in the South? Is there anything that needs healing/changing in the South?
4. **Turn West.** Ask: which image represents the West? How do I feel in the West? What is my task right now in the West? Is there anything I need to change in the West?
5. **Turn North.** Ask: which image represents the North for me? How do I feel in the North? What is my task right now in the North? Is there anything that needs changing in the North?
6. **Turn East.** Ask: which image represents the East? How do I feel in the East? What is my task right now in the East? Is there anything that needs changing in the East?
7. **Centre.** Let it all go. Stay for a while in the centre and experience the calmness of the centre. Whilst the wheel of life is turning, you can stay calmly in the centre.

8. **Finish.** Write down what you remember. Thank spirit. Dismantle the wheel.

This exercise lends itself to a second round. Travel around the wheel again, as before, and ask in each direction: How can I change what needs changing? Again, come back to the stillness in the centre at the end.

Exercise: Touching on deeper life questions- the dream

An interesting journey around the wheel is to touch on more existential questions. The following is a simple exercise, which works well when it is set up in the right way. I would only advise you attempt it if your client is ready and if you can spend time setting up a wheel in a ceremonial way, call in spirit and lead the client into an altered state before instructing her to turn in each direction, asking the specific questions:

Example

1. **South**: Who am I?
2. **North**: What is my true work?
3. **West**: What is my source of power. Where do I come from? How do I manifest?
4. **East**: What is my direction? Where am I going? For what service has spirit given birth to me?

Example

1. **East**: For what service / purpose has spirit given birth to me
2. **West**: How do I manifest this?
3. **South**: Which emotions do I need to bring to the fore to achieve this?
4. **North**: Which work would best align me with spirit's intent for me?

Ask the client to get images as well as words, hunches and feelings in relation to the question. The overall picture will emerge.

The Circle

The directions on the wheel are connected via a circle, which is a developmental map where we travel from birth (East) via our childhood (South) to middle age (West) and old age (North). From East to West our life's journey is often fairly unconscious – we are born, go through childhood, education, youth and find a job, partner-up, have children - then we hit the West, where we encounter the so-called 'midlife crisis'. The West asks us to introspect and become conscious of our life's path, creating meaning, purpose and include the spiritual. If we don't do this, we will not reach the 'wise' North, but will lead fairly meaningless lives from then onwards.

The circle is an interesting tool to work with, as we go through this journey daily, with every task we undertake. We can, for instance, take a snapshot where we are and what's going with every task and we will find, that we often get 'stuck' in the emotional South, without growing through the introspective West, unable to complete in the North. We all have experienced this: we have an idea in the east and begin to work at it until our wounded, insecure emotional South bombards us with self-doubts and anxieties, immediately supported by our 'unsorted North' with negative thought processes. This is where we usually stop and the idea never manifests in the West or completes in the North. Or we find that we are 'well developed' in one direction, but lack in another: we have many ideas in the East but we haven't got the discipline of the 'wise adult' in the North. Or we have a great work ethic, but lack the passion of the South, the creative drive of the East. All such issues can be addressed via the wheel.

Exercise: Travelling around the circle

You can take a snapshot about the client's life journey and find the 'stumbling blocks and obstacles' or 'where they are stuck'. You can use any task the client is not completing / attempting / or doubts they have about their abilities:

East: Addressing the creative spark

South: Addressing the emotional

West: Working with introspection

North: Working with beliefs and the 'wise adult'

You can do this with clients either using journeys or a journey around the wheel.

The Diagonals

The diagonals of the wheel, are balancing opposites, consisting of two axis.

North/South is the personal axis. The intelligent, thinking, skillful adult needs the emotional, playful, delighted and wondrous child, and vice versa, to achieve balance. The emotional South, disconnected from the wise mental adult in the North, can be self-indulgent and a prisoner of its own emotions, whilst the North can become hard and judgmental without the emotional self from the South.

East/West is the spiritual axis. The East is illumination, ascent, inspiration, creativity and spirit. The West is the physical, shadow, introspection, decent and earth soul. Without the West the East is 'directionless spiritual energy' or can be 'ungrounded self-serving and ego-centric spirituality' because the introspection and shadow work in the West has been neglected. Without the East, achievement in the West can be meaningless, dis-satisfying and based on hollow, material aspirations.

Balancing the 'Inner Beings'

We all suffer, to a lesser or greater extent, from the imbalance of the so-called four 'Shamanic Shields of Balance', two on the West/East axis and two on the North/South axis. Whilst western therapeutic practices are well equipped to work with the North/South axis of the wheel, the inner child and the inner adult, it rarely addresses the East/West axis, which represents, when we use the concept of shields, the inner opposite gender spirit child in the East and the inner opposite gender adult in the West. We achieve inner balance if we integrate all four. The centre point of the two axes, where they meet, holds the key to wholeness. To create wholeness, the East/West axis shields, need to be explored, included, brought to life and connected to the North/South axis shields.

The East shield is the inner spirit child of the opposite gender

The West shield is the inner spirit adult of the opposite gender.

The South shield is the child. It is normally of the same sex as the person

The North shield is the adult of the same gender as the person.

The East and West, the spirit shields, teach the North and South shields.

The West inner opposite sex adult is the archetypal opposite sex lover with all the qualities of the perfect mate. She/he will courtship the North, adding the spiritual dimension, the dimension of the intuitive mind.

The East child of the opposite gender is the archetypal spirit child, the spirited, adventurous, enthusiastic playmate to the South that teaches the wounded South how to get back into the spirit-magical, the child-magical and helps it to heal the past.

The Human Wheel: Eight Directions

What we are working towards Generally, when working with the medicine wheel, it is beneficial to keep the overall aims relating to the different directions in mind:

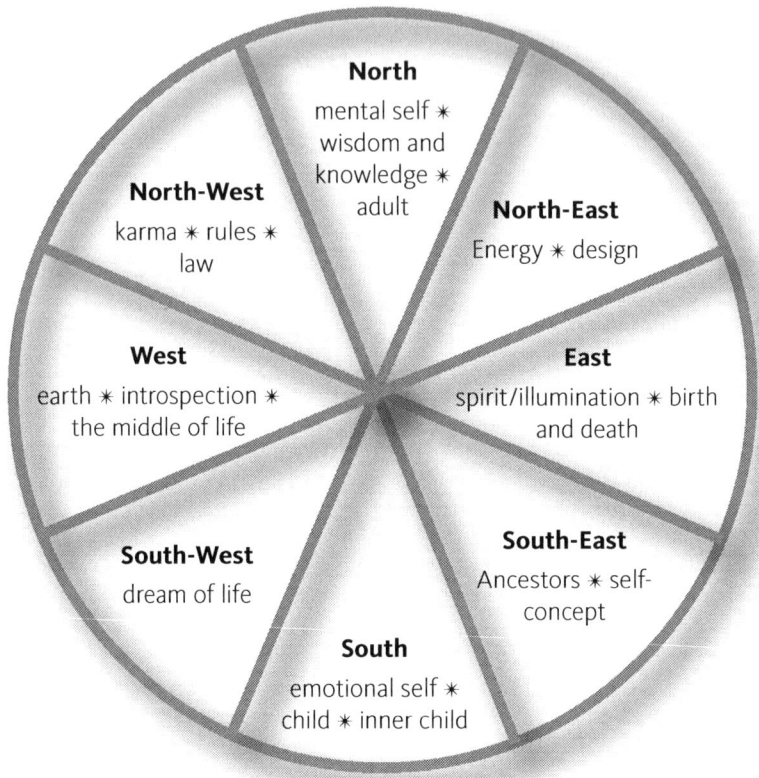

South We choose to reclaim our authentic self. We are born with trust, innocence, openness, and willingness to learn, with the ability to try things, to experience, to be playful. We are born with a range of feeling states, which we want to reclaim without being at their mercy. We open up to life and love and stop avoiding because we fear pain.

Southwest We set out to define our own dream. What we want life to be, what has meaning to us, what makes sense to us. And we begin to work, focused and consistently, setting achievable goals.

West We take responsibility and begin to actualise our dreams. We take concrete, creative action moving our dream from the imagination into the grounded place of earth. We also take responsibility for our bodies. We introspect when needed instead of avoiding. The West is the body of the mother and the child is healing by passing through the body of the 'mother'.

Northwest: We begin to implement 'sacred laws', rather than seeing the laws of society and other people's wishes and needs as our guidelines. We look at the rules and laws and ask ourselves: do they serve me, my higher goals, my higher self and with that also 'all my relations', or do they hinder me?

North We question our beliefs and ways of thinking, seeking to touch our innate sense of knowing more often, flow easier and become aware of co-incidences and 'nudges from spirit' and to try to be open to knowledge that comes our way. The North is the father and the child can heal through passing 'through the father'.

Northeast We choose from a place of balance and harmony. We design our energy to act and create, instead of react and follow. We develop focus and co-operation and remember our dream in the Southwest.

East We open our imagination to unlimited possibilities. We enter the 'realm of the magician'. We engage in spiritual practice, follow our bliss, ask for and receive spiritual vision and create lives that contribute purposefully and meaningfully to our own growth and the growth and balance of all humanity.

Southeast We are grateful to the ones that came before us, we seek to develop a self-concept, that affirms ourselves as worthy, loveable and unique co-creators of the human race, a role that is life affirming and joyful.

Centre We will find that our whole self becomes more balanced, that the conflicts lessen, that we live increasingly from our spiritual (higher) self and walk a path that has heart. We find stillness in the centre, developing a deep knowing that whilst the wheel is turning we have a still centre that is eternal.

Exercise

Using the eight directions is only advised if you feel completely comfortable with the Medicine wheel. Appropriate exercises can be found on page 233 – 237 of *Shamanism and Spirituality in Therapeutic Practice*.

Widening the Circle: Ancestors

According to shamanic thinking, the disconnection from our ancestors has produced harmful developments:

1. We have become isolated individuals without deeper roots, which contributes not only to the suffering of our psyche, but also to a disconnection from 'the whole'
2. We lost sight of the generations that will come after us and of our duty of care for them, leavig them a world that will be far from nuturing, if at all habitable.
3. We are not receiving the help and guidance from our ancestors in spirit, which would enable us to see further and deeper.

According to indigenous and shamanic cosmology, ancestors are 'part of the field and of our field', part of the mystical, that we have increasingly deadened within us. Not acknowledging the mystical and ancestors leads, according to indigenous beliefs, to living one-dimensional, poor lives because. Only when we re-awaken the mystical in us as well as our connection with the ancestors will we expand by reconnecting the different worlds.

Ancestors, in a traditional sense, are people who have lived before us and are now in spirit. They are the ones that share our bloodlines, or connected to us via 'place' and, if one subscribes to certain theories, the ones that form part of our soul groups. The further we go back in time, the more common ancestors we encounter.

In indigenous cultures it is the responsibility of the ancestor to hold the memories and wisdom gained from the past back to the dawn of humankind. It is the responsibility of the living to achknowledge the importance of the ancestors, to learn from their mistakes and create change. It is in this sense that indigenous cultures revere their ancestors, use them as role models, are in contact with them, utilise them as helping spirits, learn from them and live with them on a daily basis.

Ancestors in spirit hold the wisdom and memories of humankind, and therefore they can be role models, advisors and helping forces.

Differentiations

In shamanism, we differentiate between indigenous cultures and our own when it comes to ancestors.

Most indigenous traditions distinguish between ancestors that have successfully made the transition to the spirit world and the ones that 'didn't make it'. They are often referred to as ghosts and this term is not positive. Ancestors can only be wise, according to most indigenous beliefs, when they are in spirit form. Ancestors that didn't make it into the spirit world are stuck in the 'world between', where they do not belong and have a negative influence on the living. They need to be helped to reach the other side, a job for the experienced shaman, the so-called psycho-pomp. This is about the only context in which we hear the word 'ancestral healing' within indigenous shamanism.

In contemporary western shamanism, our focus is also directed onto 'ancestral healing': we have now many ancestors that don't make it to the other side, as we lack rituals and ceremonies, which help to guide the spirits over.

Over the last two millennia there have been more and more people who 'didn't live well'. Living well, in a traditional sense, means walking a path with honour, being embedded into a community, being a free human, taking responsibility for actions and rules, keeping one's affairs in order and leave a world to future generations, which is better, rather than worse. In theory, people who don't live well, can't die well, meaning that some of them hang around as ghosts, clinging on to life. Even if they don't linger, all of them pass on negative energetic (memory) patterns to their descendants.

Over the last millenia we fought devastating wars, uprooted many people, produced slavery, created starving populations, suppressed whole peoples or wiped them out, destroyed natural communities, habitats and boundaries, persecuted an enormous amount of people and produced many children that were either orphaned, enslaved and/or treated badly.

In shamanic terms, all of the above groups create energy fields that are detrimental to mankind and by now we have created vast numbers of such fields that need clearing. Clearing such energy fields can be challenging work and needs training.

Incorporating Ancestral Work into Therapy

Ancestral healing, which is the domain of experienced practitioners in shamanism, can be incorporated to a certain extent into therapeutic practise, although in more individualised and somehow rather mild forms.

Clearing patterns

Clients usually identify patterns relatively easily if they can look back two or three generations and/or develop an awareness for the patterns that repeat themselves in their own lives. Such patterns can be indicators of unresolved issues in ancestral lines and can be found in addictions and dependencies, in physical ailmentsof a psychosomatic nature, in relationships, in issues of power and control, in how women and children are treated and so on and so forth. We can also identify patterns that might be intergenerational by developing an awareness of what repeats itself in our lives and seems to resist change, no matter how much effort or therapy we throw at it.

Exercise: Journeying to the source

1. Identify the pattern

2. Prepare for a shamanic journey

3. Intent "I am going to journey to find the source for this pattern in my ancestral line and ask for ways to clear it. I ask my power animal, spirit helpers and well meaning ancestors to accompany me on the journey and to help me."

4. Once the client finds the source, she asks what she has to do to heal it, or to finish the business or break the pattern. Leave it up to the client to ask the guides how to do the clearing and healing. They usually know.

5. She most certainly will come across different ancestors or times when the pattern was repeated during the journey. Clear the patterns on each level on the way up.

Integration When the client is back in normal consciousness in your consulting room you can begin to cognitively integrate and to use your usual means to help the client change the pattern in her here-and-now life. In my experience, this will now be easier, after the ancestral lines have been addressed and an understanding has been developed via the shamanic journey.

Exercise: Timeline

This is a combination of an NLP timeline with a shamanic journey. Explain the concept to your client.

1. Identify the pattern

2. Ask the client to keep the issue or pattern firmly in mind and call in their spirit helpers.

3. Establish timeline

4. Use trance induction or a drumbeat and ask the client to imagine that they float above the timeline, through their ancestors lives back through time. I then ask them to stop and observe from above every time they see or sense that the pattern we are exploring has been present. I keep the client dissociated on the level above the timeline, asking him to describe to me what he sees or senses (I take Notes).

5. Keep going until he reaches the generation when the pattern was formed. Ask the client to step into the timeline, making sure that his guide and other helpers are with him, and to find out what he needs to do to heal or resolve the issue.

6. When the healing at the source is completed, instruct the client to float above the timeline again and we repeat the 'healing and resolving' in the same fashion all the way up the line, stepping (re-associating) into the time line, clearing the pattern, before floating up again, forward in time to the next event and so on.

Ceremony/ritual for letting go/integrating

I always take time to create a ritual/ceremony with my client after a journey or a timeline-clearing of ancestral patterns. If you work in a time-restricted fashion, you might have to do this in the next session. Most of the time I use a 'letting go' ritual. The pattern that needs to be let go will be embodied by creating a drawing or a piece of craft or sometimes, if time is of the essence, I ask my client to go into the garden and find something that symbolises the pattern. I then create a fire ceremony with the clients as described. Ancestral spirits are very powerful helpers as they have a direct connection to the client. I find that any ceremony is stronger when the ancestral spirits are called in.

Connecting with spirit ancestors

From the shamanic viewpoint it is vital to be connected with those ancestors that are in spirit and can be helping us on a daily basis. I have used ancestral connecting beneficially with groups and with individual clients. It might surprise you to learn that this connecting work was felt especially beneficial by people who had survived childhood abuse or neglect, or those who had been adopted or suffered the loss of parents. Many people seem to think that things get worse, the further we go back in time. From my experience, I disagree. There is, in every line or network of ancestors, at least one ancestor that clients cannot only identify with, but use as a role model and a model of aspiration. I have never met a client who couldn't connect positively with at least one ancestor and the relief is tangible, especially for clients who have had abusive experiences, or experiences of neglect, or both, from their parents. It is a well-documented fact that a relationship with one non-abusive significant adult, such as a grandparent, in an abuse survivors' childhood has a positive impact. Something similar applies to distant ancestral connections.

Exercises: connecting with ancestors

1. There are many ways to conenct with ancestors. A good first step is to do a shamanic journey with the intent "I am going to journey to the upper wolrd, to meet a helping ancestor spirit". Always ask the ancestor for his / her name and give thanks to them for being part of your life. The one can communicate with the ancestor, ask questions and more.

2. A very rewarding journey can be had when formulating the intent "I am going to journey back in time to find an ancestor that can be a role-model for me". Most people have to journey way back in time. Or "'I want to meet an ancestor that lived a life worth living, a life that was satisfying, had a worthwhile purpose and left the ancestor feeling content when he or she died.'

Once the client has found this special ancestor I advise them to have a chat, to make a connection and to bring the qualities of that ancestor back into the 'here and now' as – and I stress this – those qualities are theirs by right as they form part of their genetic make up.

3. We can also conenct with ancestors via the medicine wheel, focussing on the South/East, the place of the ancestors.

4. Another way is to represent the ancestors on the altar and then meditate in

front of it, asking to be connected with a helping ancestral spirit. Some people come up with an image, some will get hunches, insights and sudden energetic experiences.

Generally speaking, ancestoral spirits should be communicated with, honoured via a place on the altar, asked for help when appropriate and used as guiding teachers.. Usually, I also advise them to craft something that symbolises this ancestor and their qualities and to bring it with them to the next session. I will then work with the piece and also encourage them to put it on the altar so that the ancestors who have positive associations for the client are re-presented and present. Ancestors which are role-models or close guides ancestors should be contacted whenever clients feel the need and can also be used during sessions.

Travelling Home: Re-Connecting with Nature

The most insightful teachings we receive from indigenous spiritual teachers are informed by their intimate knowledge of nature and their intense connection to it. Shamanism tells us that nature is one of the best healing and teaching environments, available to all of us and free of charge – a notion confirmed by contemporary research. Shamanic practitioners will spend time in nature whenever they feel the need. They travel into nature to be alone, to heal, to revitalize and re-energise their powers, to reconnect with their initiation commitments, to converse with natural spirit allies and helpers, to be inspired and to generally fill themselves with the connection to 'all there is', with the sacred, so that they can come back to the job with more strength, power and balance.

It is not easy to transfer the nature teachings, tools and techniques used by shamanic practitioners into a consulting room. However, it is vital that professionals understand how our separation from nature has greatly contributed to the disenchantment of our psyche and to the imbalance we experience, how profoundly the natural environment can nurture and balance us emotionally and mentally and give our bodies pleasure and enchant our souls, and that we therefore encourage clients to re-connect with it.

Encouraging clients to 'get out and involve themselves in the natural world' contributes positively to the therapeutic process. It enhances physical, emotional and spiritual well-being. It will contribute to narrowing the gap between our lives spent mostly in artificial environments, from urban sprawls to cyberspace, and our longing for something more simple and natural. It will help us to reveal the inner, that which is beyond what we access in daily life because nature, if we sharpen our awareness, reflects back our most intense fears and also our highest joys. It will re-instate a sense of the power, beauty and awesomeness of basic life forces and of ourselves. Nature calms the mind, opens the senses and nourishes us on deep levels. As nature inherently leads to connection with the deepest parts of our being, where self-knowledge, inner balance, and inherent healing abilities already exist, we become naturally more peaceful, wise and healthy. In fact, I would postulate that wilderness resonates on the level of soul. It will lower the barriers we have erected between the natural world and ourselves, which keeps us disconnected from the longings of our souls to be known by us. Our soul is, after all, our inner wilderness, that intra-psychic land, of which most of us only experience glimpses until we have the courage to attempt the hero's journey. (for research data see chapter 16 of *Shamanism and Spirituality in Therapeutic Practice*).

In this context it is interesting to note that no client of mine ever visualised a busy shopping street or his work place or his local pub or a club as a place of power, refuge or sanctuary. The vast majority of clients of all age groups visualise a place in nature when asked to find their special place, normally one containing the elements of water, earth, air and fire, in form of the sun, which they describe as calming, healing and nurturing. Parks, a therapist and healer from the Association for the Advancement of Psychosynthesis reflects that an astonishing quantity of nature symbolism in form of animals, plants and minerals occur in healing and self-realization experiences and that nature herself can therefore be seen as the universal healer.

Helping Clients to Re-connect with Nature

Contemporary shamanic practitioners will work in nature with a range of means and tools. The most profound, transformational experiences can be had during vision quests, especially when experienced facilitators conduct them in a wild environment. Vision quests, lead us into the wilderness, on our own, for days and nights. The sweat lodge ceremony is also conducted in- and connected to- nature and so are most medicine wheel ceremonies. Solstice-, Sun-Dance-, medicine plant ceremonies and many other ceremonies and rituals are performed outside. Nature awareness walks, meditation exercises, the burial of the warrior, training for seeing and connecting with the essences/spirits of plants, rocks and trees are all part of the 'shamanic nature repertoire'. In fact, the entire middle world, the world around us, is where the shaman communicates with the essence aspects of nature. As all things are seen as having a spiritual essence, we therefore have the ability to connect with all of nature, communicate with it and learn from it.

Education

Even if we cannot transfer nature exercises easily into contemporary therapeutic practice, we can educate clients by making them aware of the benefits I have listed in chapter 16 of my book. We can encourage outdoor activities and outdoor sports, rather than suggesting exercising in the gym, where most of us put on our headphones and either watch TV or listen to music to overcome the boredom of the treadmill or the rowing machine. Another way is to encourage clients to replace the 'city-break' with a 'nature-break' or a 'walking break', or to engage in one of the many nature activities on offer, such as participating in wilderness camps, nature foraging courses or nature survival courses, or learning how to cultivate vegetable gardens and so forth. I personally would also encourage certain clients, especially those who need struggle to find their path in life, to consider a vision quest, or some outdoor ceremony, provided the facilitator is experienced, trained and provides integration afterwards.

Becoming conscious of the gifts of nature and developing gratitude

An easy, yet essential, shamanic practice is to become more conscious of nature's life-giving and life-sustaining forces, reminding ourselves that we wouldn't be alive without her, and develop gratitude and appreciation. This works especially well for clients who feel that there is not much in their lives, which they want to be grateful about. Each breath we take, every drop of water we drink, and most of the foods we eat, come from nature. The joy we feel when the rays of the sun touch us, the refreshing coolness of the wind on our skin, the sound of a river that calms us – no matter what it is – these blessings and so many more all come from nature. Encourage clients to go outside and let a sense of gratitude develop, without forcing it, can be healing.

Exercise: Being seen by mother nature

A powerful, quick way of reconnecting with nature is to instruct clients to be seen by nature. We have a tendency to 'look at', forgetting that we are also 'being looked at'. You can give this exercise as homework, or, if your practice is set in an adequate environment, you can do this exercise at the end of a session. I have used it with individual clients many times, normally at the end of the session, especially when the session was emotionally demanding or distressing. I usually allocate 15 minutes for it.

Instruct the client to

1. Go outside, taking a note pad.

2. Find a spot that feels right, close your eyes and breathe deeply for a few minutes.

3. With your eyes closed, imagine that you are seen by Mother Nature. Imagine that she is looking at you, as one of her cherished children, with love.

4. Trust your inner clock, open your eyes again when you feel the urge to do so, and write down what your experienced – thoughts, feelings, sensory experiences, ideas.

If this exercise works for a specific client, ask them to repeat it twice a week. With time, the connection deepens and the positive loving regard of nature will work its magic.

Exercise: Awareness walks

Most therapists will recommend exercise. Exercise is good for the depressed client, for the anxious individual, for the grieving client, for the person with low self-esteem, for the stressed-out high-achiever and for the over-weight. We could encourage clients to take walks between sessions. A nice way to turn a walk into something more than physical exercise is to use it to sharpen awareness for- and connection with - nature.

Ask your client to do two 20-minute walks between sessions, either in a park, if you work in an urban area, or along a river or somewhere else in nature.

Instruct your client to

1. Listen intently for 5 minutes, noting all the sounds.
2. Experience / feel the sensations produced by air, wind, warmth, coolness, rain, sun for 5 minutes.
3. Notice for 5 minutes what is around them - the trees and plants and all the 'wildlife they can spot'
4. Connect for 5 minutes with the ground, bringing the awareness to the feet and notice, the connection to the earth.

Ask your client to take a few minutes afterwards, when back home or at the end of the walk, to contemplate and write down whatever comes to his mind about the walk. You can use this in the next session.

Exercise: Let 'something find you' walks

Another awareness walk, which will connect clients with a world beyond their normal perception,(in shamanic terms with 'the spirits'), is to 'be found by something'.

Instruct your client to

1. Walk relaxed, consciously and silently

2. State, after a few minutes of walking, an intent along the lines of 'I ask for whatever wants to find me, to find me.'

3. After stating this intent a few times, the client just keeps walking with awareness, being assured, something will find them (this usually comes in a surprising form, is needed in their life and captures their attention).

Again, it is beneficial to write the experience down and use it in the next session.

There are many ways to create 'awareness walks'. You can adjust the concept to your client's personality and to the condition you are treating. It is important, though, that awareness and focus is directed onto nature, not the client's inner state. The focus on nature will create a resonating inner state, which, if that's what you want, can then be therapeutically explored and worked with.

Connecting with the Spirits of Nature

Before shamanic practitioners begin to work in a place, they honour its spirit. During the honouring they will get to know the spirit of the place and often will be given signs about the place, its energy and what is required to work beneficially within it.

The spirit of a place consists of many layers and ingredients, including all the human imprints. But, as we are connecting with nature, we use the indigenous definition of spirit and spirituality of 'place', which is based on the ecology of a place: every landscape or place is a web and together they form the great web of Being and Becoming. So it is the spirit of this smaller web within the large web of life that you want to get to know and honour.

Exercise: Honouring the spirit of a place

1. Go to a place in nature.
2. Still yourself
3. Close your eyes. Ask the spirit of the place to connect with you or call it with a drum or rattle.
4. Listen and be aware: you will get hunches, images, maybe words, a sudden knowing, a feeling.
5. When you feel that you are connected, ask the spirit of the place any question you choose and note the answer.
6. Leave something to honour the spirit or conduct a little ceremony.

Exercise: Connecting with the spirit of one's own place

If clients are in harmony with the spirit of their own place they will find that life runs more smoothly and that the place will support them. If you help a client for the first time, it is beneficial to journey to the spirit of their own place, which can be done in the consulting room. Later they can just briefly tune into it, whenever necessary.

1. Intent: "I am journeying to meet the spirit of this place and ask him/her to advise me how to best be in this place and serve it so that it also serves me."
2. Let the journey unfold. Write it down afterwards.

This is an exercise I really would advise people to do if they don't feel 'right' in their own homes, because it's astonishing how much information they receive. They will be shown which adjustments to make, or which energies are strong and which need strengthening or clearing.

Connecting with the spirit aspects of all living things

In shamanism we connect with and get to know the 'the spirit aspects' of living things in nature, which also helps us to get to know ourselves and strengthen our own spiritual aspect. These exercises are only advised if you work more in an ecological or deeper way. As a first step I would advise you to help clients connect with the essences – the spirit aspects – of trees, plants, rocks, mountains, forests and rivers or those of the elements, such as water, earth, fire, air.

Exercise: Connecting outside

Instruct your client to

1. Go outside. Find a spot that feels right or go to the tree, plant, river or whatever you want to connect with.

2. Call in spirit.

3. Go into a meditative trance: breathe, rattle, drum or sing and close your eyes.

4. Tell the tree (plant, rock) that you would like to connect.

5. Imagine that you are connecting in whatever form feels right to you.

6. Be patient. Listen deeply. Just stay connected and become aware of images, hunches, sounds, feelings, sudden insights.

7. You will know when you have finished for the time being. Thank the tree and write down what you remember.

Connecting via the shamanic journey

Another way is through the shamanic journey. Your intent will be: "I am journeying to the middle world to connect with the essence of the tree. I ask the tree to teach me." Then let the journey unfold.

Daily Nature Exercises at Home

Mediations

Clients who meditate, practice yoga or tai-chi or are engaged in any other regular spiritual practice should be encouraged to add the quality of nature to their activities whenever this is possible. Engaging in mindfulness meditation practices near a stream, river, rock or under a tree can add a wider dimension, with astonishing results.

Brief ceremonies

Another way in which we can bring the healing and connecting qualities of nature into the therapeutic process is through designing brief ceremonies that clients can perform daily in their back yard, on the balcony or in the garden. The first step is to create an altar representing the elements. I discuss this with clients – not everybody, but the ones that are open to such suggestions - during the session. I talk to them about taking a walk somewhere to find four pieces that represent air, fire, water and earth for them and suggest that they then create a small space somewhere in the open and arrange the pieces, either in a way that just feels right or in the four directions of the wheel. I also ask them to find a centre piece that represents that 'which always is and will always be'. A daily small blessing of the elements or a brief meditation or a few minutes of calm thankfulness is then recommended. Give suggestions, but in the end leave it up to the client's imagination.

Greeting the directions

An enchanting way in which we can work outside involves the directions of the wheel. Every shamanically-orientated facilitator and every indigenous shaman will, in one form or another, honour the directions, calling them in before they work, asking them for blessings and so on. It seems that the directions resonate with us, once we begin to work with them. The easiest way to begin is to greet them in the morning. One can simple stand outside, close one's eyes and turn into each direction - the south, north, east, west - and then to the sky and the earth, expressing a greeting. For example, turn east and greet the sun; turn south and greet the plants and the water; turn west and greet the earth; turn north and greet the air, and then look up and greet all there is above and look down and greet all there is below.

One can go further and ask each direction for a piece of advice for the day or give thanks, if it's evening. Over time we feel that we begin to connect with our daily environment differently. We begin to experience it in a more natural and spatially wider sense, feeling more embedded in it.

There are many more ways to get to know the natural world and connect with her via simple exercises during walks such as exploring the mysteries of the seasons, learning to read terrains, getting to know different plants and herbs, finding answers to questions and so on. Encouraging clients to make a start by connecting, developing awareness and communicating with nature will greatly enhance their well-being and contribute developing a sense of being embedded in – and part of - something bigger and wider than themselves.

Notes

Basic Skills and Tools

Working with Spirit: Calling the Spirit Forces

A Sense of the Sacred

Working with Space

Sacredness and Wholeness of the Client

Axis Mundi, Cosmic Worlds & Levels of Human Perception

Spirit Allies

The Shamanic Journey

Journeys of Retrieval and Connection

Journeys of Learning or Guidance

Soul Loss and Soul Retrieval

Ceremony and Ritual

The Medicine Wheel: Life in Circles and Cycles

The Human Aspects of the Wheel: Four Directions

The Circle

The Diagonals

The Human Wheel: Eight Directions

Widening the Circle: Ancestors

Travelling Home: Re-Connecting with Nature

Connecting with the Spirits of Nature

Daily Nature Exercises at Home

Based on the books

Christa Mackinnon (2012) *Shamanism and Spirituality in Therapeutic Practice* Jessica Kingsley Publishers, London & Philadelphia

Christa Mackinnon (2016) *Shamanism: Awaken and Develop the Shamanic Force Within* Hay House, London & Carlsbad CA

Drumming Download for journeying

You can request the link for a 20 minute drumming download via my website contact page: www.christamackinnon.com

Christa Mackinnon is a psychologist, family counsellor, clinical hypnotherapist, university lecturer, shamanic practitioner and author, who worked as a therapist, trainer and lecturer internationally for over 25 years and has learned from shamans and spiritual teachers in South America, the USA, Asia and Europe. She now facilitates mainly training courses and workshops, combining indigenous spiritual traditions with contemporary therapeutic approaches, and writes and speaks extensively about the subject. She is the author of *Shamanism and Spirituality in Therapeutic Practice* (Jessica Kingsley Publ. 2012) and *Shamanism: Awaken and Develop the Shamanic Force Within* (Hay House, 2016).

Printed in Great Britain
by Amazon